ARE WE *REALLY* TEACHING RELIGION?

ARE WE *REALLY* TEACHING RELIGION?

By F. J. SHEED

SHEED AND WARD
NEW YORK

CONTENTS

NOTE

A couple of summers ago I spoke to the Teaching Nuns of Ireland, gathered in annual conference in Dublin, upon the topic "Are We Really Teaching Religion?" Rough copies of the talk were made and widely circulated. Teachers wrote asking for the elucidation of certain points. It seemed simplest, in the end, to make this formal publication of what I originally said, together with a Note containing most of the elucidations asked for. I hope that this pamphlet may be of use not only to teachers, but to parents: unless there is co-operation between them, religious instruction will go limpingly.

F.J.S.

ARE WE *REALLY*
TEACHING RELIGION?

THE subject of this lecture is not of my choosing. It was not *I* who decided that I should speak to *you* on the teaching of Religion. The topic came from yourselves. I take it that what you wanted was an outside look at the question. After all, you spend your lives teaching Religion. It might be interesting, or at the very worst amusing, to hear what an amateur has to say on the same subject, and it is really from that point of view that I am going to speak. If anything I say should seem to you to be critical of the teaching of Religion in Catholic schools, at least I am not criticizing *you*, because I don't know you. I have never heard you teach, I have never been in a school in Ireland. All I know of Ireland in this particular matter is that my ancestors learnt the Faith there, and I still have it. Any criticisms I make are based upon my experience of the countries I frequent. So that from your point of view the question should be altered to read "Are *they* really teaching religion?" You can compare anything I may have to say in criticism of the situation in these other countries with your own knowledge of what happens here, and see how far any of it applies to you. At the end you will perhaps be giving thanks to God that you are not as one of these.

1

But criticism will be incidental, not my main business. I shall, indeed, not attempt to answer the question you have set me, but only to state the principles in the light of which it must be answered. I am aware that much that I am going to say will seem to you elementary, you will wonder why I should bother to say things so obvious. But much may strike you as fantastic, unrelated to the prosaic realities of teachers, pupils and classrooms. After all you are teachers, I am not. You know the story—I heard it first as a boy and have heard it scores of times since—of the young priest, newly ordained, preaching a sermon in a great parish church on Marriage, and the two old ladies leaving the church after, one saying to the other: "I wish I knew as little about it as he does." And I imagine as I go on talking about the teaching of Religion in schools, you will think back over the years of agony you have devoted to precisely that, and smile wryly at my happy innocence. I am aware of all that and yet I am quite shameless in accepting your invitation. As it happens, I *have* taught in schools—I did so as a young man in Australia, with my elders and betters telling me I would never make a teacher; and since then I have taught Religion in a surprising number of schools, at evening classes, in college courses, in study clubs, and on street corners. All the same it is not from such teaching experience that I shall draw what I am going to say. The real value of *any* education begins to show ten years after. This paper is based upon discussions of religion I have had with thousands of men and women who went to Catholic schools when young. What they know now is the test of what they were taught then. That is the experience on which I shall be drawing for the next hour or so.

I

I take it, as regards the *aim* of the teaching of Religion in Catholic schools, that we are agreed on something like this:

that the indispensable minimum is that the Catholics coming out of our schools should emerge with a tremendous devotion to Christ, Our Lord, with an awareness of Him, a considerable knowledge of His Life and Personality, and a desire to increase that knowledge; if they have got that, they are all right; even if they have got nothing else, they are still all right, they will come to very little harm. But if they have not, all other excellences don't do them a great deal of good. None the less, the other excellences are excellences and to be striven for. It should surely be the aim of religious teaching that, by the time the pupils leave, they should have learned the great doctrines of the Church, up to the level of their capacity to absorb them at that age and with the somewhat scanty experience of life they have so far had; and that they should have acquired such a liking for the doctrines that they will want to go on studying them, roughly pari passu with their experience of life.

Let me take three or four questions that might test how far these aims had been achieved—not necessarily the most important that could be asked, but easy to answer with a yes or no, and in their own way pretty decisive:

(i) Are Catholics, by and large, so equipped with knowledge of the doctrines of the Church, that if some outsider came along and wanted enlightenment, the first educated Catholic he came to would give it to him, would really expound the Church's main doctrines in such a way that the enquirer would think the matter worth pursuing with a priest? Would he, by the time he reached the priest, already have learnt a great deal?

(ii) Do Catholics really want to go to Heaven? I don't mean, do they want to go at once. I mean have they, with all their love of life, the life of here and now, a real desire to go to Heaven—not simply a desire to avoid hell, but an actual desire, knowing what Heaven is, to embrace it? Would that be a normal state of the Catholics who have been to our schools?

(iii) Take a third quite different sort of test. Supposing one of our Catholics were to find upon the table in his bedroom a religious book, say by Dr. Leen or Monsignor Ronald Knox, and a novel—which would he pick up? I realize that there are moods in which every one of us, even you, would rather have the novel. All I mean is: are those the *only* moods that Catholics have? If so, it means they have no very vivid interest in God, in Christ, our Lord, in our Lady, in all the major facts of reality.

(iv) One further test: A Catholic receives the gifts of truth and life that the Church has to give him, through Christ our Lord. Is he in a kind of anguish at the thought that there are others who know nothing of these gifts and are not receiving them? Can he take it quietly, can he go about his business and only occasionally say: "Poor fellows, they are unlucky"? Or is it a matter of anguish that fellow human beings should be starved of the gifts of truth and life that Christ wanted them to have? Is he as much concerned at that fact and conscious that he ought to be doing something about it, as he would be if he heard that fellow creatures lacked bread? If he is not, then it means that bread has a more real value for him than the truth and the Sacraments. This may be so, even if, as a practising Catholic, he frequents the Sacraments. There may still be a good deal of routine in his own regular Catholic life—though of course, by the mercy of God, that routine is a life-giving routine and will lead him to salvation.

My own feeling is that we do not measure up very well to those four tests. We, as a body, with all our practice of the Catholic religion, are not alive to the Faith in that sort of way. I travel a great deal, more than most, and as a result I meet a far greater variety of people than most; and because I am known to be a Catholic publisher, I hear a great many more religious views. In the Catholic Evidence Guild, I have had thirty years of meeting the incoming members, the people who would like to be speakers. On this mass of evidence, I can only state my own conclusion that even with those who are really devoted Catholics, religion has not for the most part *taken* in that kind of way—the Sacraments, yes, thank God; the Mass, yes, thank God; but you don't feel the whole Catholic outlook on life profoundly comprehended or really very much adverted to: and of course sadly large numbers have dropped Mass and Sacraments altogether. From meeting so many of my fellow Catholics, I have formed a mental picture of the Religion classes from which they have emerged. That is the basis of my talk this afternoon.

II

One begins with *the attitude of the Religion teacher*. I have masses of evidence about that. There are Catholic schools in which Religion is a poor relation on the syllabus. If there is a teacher who would startle the Government Inspector if he caught her teaching Mathematics or English or Latin or French, she is relegated to the teaching of Christian Doctrine; the principle apparently being that the Diocesan Inspector is made of sterner stuff than the Government Inspector and does not startle so easily. You may not believe it, but I have seen such schools.

I will say no more of these base institutions. We are talking about schools that really take Religion teaching as the primary work, the thing for which more than anything else they exist. Now the primary rule of all teaching that is supposed to affect the way in which human beings live is that the teacher is not simply handing out information like a post-office girl handing out stamps. The teacher gives *herself,* with the truth adhering. There is no way of giving the truth without giving oneself. There must be actual self-donation of the teacher, and the truth somehow goes with that self-donation. Everything I have to say assumes that *that* is taken for granted by every teacher of Religion in a Catholic school.

But let us say two further things. First—if the teacher regards the Religion class as a kind of sacramental, a kind of sub-sacrament, then it would be quite impossible for her either to have any slackness in preparing to give it, or any dishonesty in giving it. It would be quite unthinkable, it would be, in its own sort of way, not exactly a sacrilege—it certainly is not—but something moving in that direction. When I mention dishonesty in giving the lesson, there flash through my mind incidents people have told me of, occasions in class where the Religion teacher tried to bluff when she did not know, or, being caught out in ignorance, lost her temper. Now I know that these things have been exaggerated, time does exaggerate them. But after all, you as teachers know that you live permanently in the appalling certainty that all your lapses are going to be exaggerated. So you have to be terribly careful not to have lapses.

Second — as the Catholic looks back over his Religion classes, there should be no memory of harshness to stain his devotion to religion; whatever may be true in the other classes, there should be no harshness in this class. The amount of resentment one finds over things that took place thirty years ago, a resentment which is sometimes profoundly serious, which sometimes means even the dropping of the practice of the faith, is amazing. I have been in school myself, and I know that there are teachers who are positive lions— their slightest whisper is a roar. I remember a particular teacher who roared so effectively that I will never open a book in his subject again, willingly. Be a lion, if you must, in the other classes, but be a lamb in the Religion class. If children learn nothing else, or retain nothing else, from their Religion classes, let them learn and retain that religion is love. If all the rest goes, let that stay. And it does seem to me that a teacher should examine his conscience to see if there be any incident that might have dimmed the realization in anybody that religion is love. I know that, as a street corner speaker for the Catholic Evidence Guild, I examine mine on that point. There have been occasions when I was sarcastic to a questioner. I have not flogged myself for it, though I should have, because my sarcasm stands between that questioner and the love of God, and I put it there. The love of God cannot be taught with a snarl or a sneer; and if the love of God is not taught religion is not. It would be wonderful if everybody coming from a Catholic school could look back on the Religion classes and say: "They were different. Even Sister So-and-So was a Christian in the Religion class!"

Now I know I speak of something that is your affair and not mine, but I think I would not punish children in the Religion classes if they did not do their homework. I think I would, as far as is humanly possible, leave compulsion out of the Religion class. It is not the same as the other classes. I would not do anything that would give them a resentment toward me, which they would proceed to attach to religion. Try to persuade them, yes; get them so interested that they want to learn, yes. But not compulsion. In the matter of behaviour, you cannot of course have the place turned into a bear garden. But my tendency would be not to punish them in the Religion class for any sort of misbehaviour that did not tend to disrupt the class. If they are merely day-dreaming, try to be more interesting than their dreams. And, for most faults, use the Religion class to illustrate the value of forgiveness up to seventy times seven. Religion class would be a wonderful place for that.

I do not think the Religion class should be a class at all. It is not simply part of school work. It happens to be in the same building; it happens to be run by the same people; but it is not part of school life, it is something much more profound than that. The teacher in the Religion class is not exactly there as a school mistress, she is there as a maturer member of the Catholic Church, trying to convey, to less mature members, just what treasures the Church has. Compulsion is a thing that rankles. You would be amazed at the number of grown-up Catholics who resent having had to go to Holy Communion with all the others. And this for two reasons. Number one: in many cases, it meant sacrilege. They had not the nerve to stand out, they had not the nerve to go to Confession over some sin or other, they had a bad conscience. Not only that, it caused them to associate Communion with a great mass-movement, without any personal choice at all. Consequently, once they left school, they lacked the mass-movement and they gave up Communion. It is the same with this question of religion when it is thought of as part of school life. I have seen it to the point where it is almost heartbreaking. Children, so devoted, so devout, at school. And the moment they leave school they drop religion, because religion was simply one more part of school life. Anything we can do to make children feel that their Religion class is not just part of going to school would be wonderful.

III

It is a commonplace that the teacher in the class room teaches in two ways. She teaches by what she *is*, and she teaches by what she *says*. And everybody knows that the first sort of teaching—teaching by what you are—lasts longer, is the more permanent. But not for that reason would you neglect the teaching by what you say. Any teacher who says to herself: "What I *am* is what matters to the class, not what I *say*, so I will improvise as I go along," is a charlatan. Surely any Catholic would feel rather that what she *is* is such a shoddy thing that she had better make up for it by a greater excellence in what she *says*. Would any of us have the nerve to sit there and say: "I am so excellent a being that what I say hardly matters, all they need do is absorb *me*"? On the contrary, the teacher really trembles at the thought that so much throughout the rest of the child's life is going to hinge upon the child's reaction to her. It cannot be helped, but it means that you have to be better than yourselves in the Religion class room.

What I am going to say next, I say with the fullest sense of responsibility. Far too many of the Religion teachers I have met have seemed to me not really competent. You will say that my experience could be of only a small proportion of all Religion teaching. That is quite true. But it is larger than most people have had. I am going to analyze my impressions so that you may judge how far the standard I am suggesting is a right standard.

It seems to me that there are two elements of intellectual competence which should be a minimum for the teaching of Religion.

(i) The teacher of Religion should be absolutely soaked in the New Testament, so that she knows what every key chapter in it is about; knows the line of thought of every book of it, could find her way about it blindfold. That seems to me an indispensable minimum and if a teacher just lets the New Testament go by, does not take too much account of it, merely looks it up when questions arise or uses it for texts to prove doctrines, then what she is really doing, by ignoring the Book, is snubbing the Author of the Book. The Author of the Book is the Holy Ghost. And if you snub the Holy Ghost, it is hard to see how you can count upon His co-operation in your class; and without His co-operation, it is hard to see how you will accomplish anything. The teaching of Religion is a kind of dialogue—I was almost going to say between the Holy Ghost and the Holy Ghost—the Holy Ghost in you helping you to say the truth, and the Holy Ghost in the child helping it to understand what you are saying. It really is your work, you are not passive, you are not nothing —but the Holy Ghost is acting in you if you let Him. The same is true of the child—the child is not passive, not nothing, but the Holy Ghost is helping it to understand what you say. Ideally, one should know the whole of the New Testament; the Gospels *must* be known thoroughly. In addition to reading the four Gospels, one should have a good Harmony of the Gospels, and live with it. That is number one of the qualifications which seem to me to be an indispensable minimum.

(ii) The teacher should be soaked also in the Church's dogmas, soaked in them in this sense that she knows them in so far as the Church has expounded them; and further, that she is possessed by them. This experience of having the dogmas of the faith come alive in the mind is a most fascinating psychological thing. It is not my business to appraise the value of teaching the words of the Catechism, but I would like to give a word of warning. The Catechism makes it possible for people to teach doctrine without knowing doctrine. But the teacher who is soaked in dogma, really afire with it, is not in the least likely to confine herself merely to a repetition of Catechism words. The very essence of being possessed by any truth at all is a desire to tell it. To be possessed by a truth and not to long to communicate it would be impossible. The mark of the teacher who is possessed by truth is an almost anguished desire to convey to others what is so rich a treasure to her.

Most of the Religious teachers I have met do not seem to be in that sense soaked in the dogmas; still fewer, one feels, are soaked in the New Testament. For the last thirty years I have been teaching the Faith at street corners. Throughout that time I have been receiving the people who join the Catholic Evidence Guild, who want to be trained as speakers, and finding out what they know. Those who come are not the worst Catholics, obviously. They would not want to speak at street corners to their fellow citizens if they were thoroughly bad Catholics. We have probably a good average lot of Catholics; some of them have just left school, some left school thirty or forty years ago, some are converts. Except for the recent converts, the effort to find what they know is very depressing. The best of them know the Catechism answers, but the moment one questions them as to the meaning of an answer, there is trouble. They can nearly always get the first answer right, but if, instead of going on to the next question, you question their answer, you find that the foundation is chaos. Among them, over the years, have been a great number of school teachers and they are just the same as the rest.

Many of those who come to us, the ones most recently at school, have been taught Apologetics and have been taught very well, though too often they have been trained to answer yesterday's questions and not today's, so that when they meet a living objector, the sword of their apologetic breaks in their hand, proves in fact to be no true sword, but only a good imitation. However that may be, there is invariably one most extraordinary thing about their Apologetics. They have learnt the *proofs* of all sorts of Catholic doctrines, but they do not know, and seem to have no desire to know, what the doctrines themselves mean: they are at once uninformed and incurious about the realities which they are so pleased to prove that the Church has.

Thus they can prove, by evidence internal and external, that the Gospels are authentic. I have hardly ever met one of them who has read the Gospels.

They can prove that the soul of man is spiritual, that man

therefore is a union of spirit and matter: but what the union means, how things so disparate are in fact united, they do not know. Over and over again, one has had some such dialogue as this: "Is the soul in every part of your body?—Yes—Is it in your thumb?—Yes—Then, if your thumb were cut off, what would happen to the soul that had been in it?" A fool of a question, perhaps. But the answers reveal that the vast majority have not a notion of what the phrase "union of spirit and matter" means, so do not know what a man is, and apparently have never even wondered.

They can prove that the Pope is infallible, but they do not know the meaning of infallibility. You can discover this by asking "Why, if the Pope is infallible, does he summon a General Council? If he cannot teach error, why have a council to prevent his teaching error?" To be unable to answer this question (which most of them are) is not to know the difference between being prevented from teaching error and being able to teach truth, and therefore not to know what Infallibility means. But they can prove it all right.

One last example: they can prove from the Gospels that Christ Our Lord is God, but they do not know the meaning of the doctrine whose truth they have so convincingly established, what it *means* that this man was God. They have not gone into it and have not any curiosity in the matter. You ask, for instance, "Did God die on the Cross?" The answer, happily, is Yes—as I have said the first answer is usually right. But if you go on and ask "What happened to the universe while God was dead?" nearly all abandon the great truth to which they have just assented, and explain that it was not God who died on the Cross but the human nature God the Son had assumed: which roughly is the Nestorian heresy, condemned at the Council of Ephesus in 431, one year before St. Patrick landed for the conversion of your ancestors and mine. The true answer, you may say, sounds not so very different from the heresy: need we bother the young with technical distinctions of this sort? But upon this distinction our redemption depends and the young are quite capable of seeing the distinction, and of rejoicing in it.

Students thus drilled in the arguments but unconcerned about the realities have not been taught by teachers soaked in the New Testament or soaked in the dogmas. They come to the Evidence Guild classes and start to learn; and you can see beginning to grow in them the excitement that is born of *a sense of being initiated into divine mysteries*—an excitement they were quite capable of having at any stage in their career. As the realization comes to life—we see this invariably—there begins also to grow the desire to communicate, to go out and tell these truths to people who have not got them: the feeling that it is intolerable that there should be anybody who has not had at least an opportunity of having them, of knowing these marvellous things. Please do not misunderstand me. I know that one can be a good Catholic, one can be saved, one can be a Saint, with very little notion of the content of Catholic doctrine. But it still remains true that, to one who loves God, every new truth learned about God is a new reason for loving Him, and it still remains true that every doctrine contains light for the mind, and nourishment for the soul, and that that light and nourishment remain locked up in it for anyone who has never been taken inside it, to see what is there.

IV

The products of our Catholic schools—ten years or more after, you understand, when I meet them—lack two things overwhelmingly. They lack the shape of reality as expressed in the dogmas, and they lack any inside knowledge of what the individual dogmas mean. A great devotion, willingness to do God's will, devotion to the Church's laws, devotion to the Sacraments, devotion to the Mass—these things are there, but side by side with a chaotic picture of what it all means.

I have already glanced at the lack of grip on individual dogmas. Take now the question of the shape of reality. Catholicism means the union of men with God in Christ. That is Catholicism, that is all of Catholicism. That is the fact they should have standing up clear and clean from all the mass of things they know. As they come through school, they have learnt a great number of things, but there is no order, no hierarchy, in the things they have learnt about the faith. They have all sorts of pious practices, good salutary practices, rubbing shoulders, so to speak, with essentials. They hardly know which is which, they are all there together in a kind of —I was going to say rag-bag, but that would be rude—they are all there in a kind of heap. The absolutely essential activities of Catholicism and the quite desirable but non-essential pious practices—all there together—the Trinity hardly larger than our Lady of Fatima! They need some framework on which they can arrange their knowledge, to which all the rest can be related, and I suggest the simple definition of Catholicism I have just quoted: the union of men with God in Christ. We are incorporated with Christ and thereby united with the Father and with one another.

The union of men with God in Christ is Catholicism; and, that being so, whatever else they are clear or vague about, whatever else they remember or do not remember, they should be absolutely clear on *what God is, what man is, what Christ is, what union is.* Those four should stand out like a great plateau—you can arrange all the other things around these. Those four they really should know. Do they know them? One small piece of evidence could obviously be collected in our churches: the sermons preached are not preached as to a congregation that knows those four things. The priests must know their people. An occasional priest might under-rate his congregation: but if the clergy as a whole preach only the simplest elements, they are surely uttering their verdict on what their people already know. They say that a dogmatic sermon would be above the heads of the congregation—the majority of whom have had anything from eight to twelve years in Catholic schools: you would think it must be very hard to be above such heads. There is indeed an astounding contrast between what the religious curriculum says is to be taught in school, and what the sermons say has been learnt.

Come back to these things—what God is, what man is, what Christ our Lord is, what union is—union with God in Christ.

V

I have been suggesting that there are two indispensable elements in Religion Really Taught (to revert to the question you set me): (1) that individual truths should be known in their inwardness, the children should be shown how to get under the skin of the doctrine to find what is there: the words of the Catechism should be broken up into their component sentences; (2) that the truths should be seen as parts of an organic whole, like features in a face, and that face should be known intimately and seen everywhere: the "shape" of reality must become a permanent mental possession, not in the sense of truths known so that one can recall them at need, but (to change the simile slightly) in the sense of major features of the landscape in which the mind is consciously living: if this is achieved, then the student will never be able to see anything without at the same time seeing God and man and Christ and the union of men with God in Christ, will never be able to judge of any problem that arises in his life without seeing it in relation to God's will and the supernatural life and the Beatific Vision. In other words he is living mentally in the real universe, which helps him morally, too: for the Laws of morality are the Laws of this *real* universe, and if one is living mentally *in* it, one sees that they are, so that intellect helps will in its struggle: whereas to be trying to obey the laws of the real universe, while not living mentally in it, casts the whole burden of virtue on the will.

That the pupils should learn to see Religion so, the teacher must already be seeing it so, and must have given endless thought to the way of sharing her vision with her pupils.

Consider the seeing it first. Any teacher of any subject must know far more than he has to impart: with knowledge it is as with the voice, you get your effects with what you are not using: the speaker at the limit of his voice, the teacher at the limit of his knowledge, each in his own way sounds thin and tinny: what is being held in reserve gives resonance to what is being used. The Religion teacher, then, will be always thrusting deeper into the inwardness of the doctrines. And she will be living ever more consciously and intensely in the seen reality: a teacher will be able to introduce the children into the world of reality in which she herself is wholly living and rejoicing to live, just as she will teach more vividly the geography of a country she has lived in and loved.

Consider now, but all too briefly, the effort of the mind to grow in the art of sharing the vision. There is, of course, the solid groundwork of teaching method. Of that I need not speak. I suggest two further points:

(i) There should be a continuous thrust of the mind, to discover less-obvious but still fascinating implications of the dogmas.

When teaching the Incarnation, for instance, of course you teach them that Christ is God, and that Christ is Man, and as they grow into the doctrine, they begin to see how marvellous a thing it is that God should have taken a human nature, made it wholly His own. But you can go further, and should invite your students to go further, especially your older students. Just think what it must have been to the Man, Christ, to know that He was God—because He had to embrace the knowledge of His own Godhead with a human intellect, a human intellect like ours. And He had to respond to it with human emotions, human emotions like ours. Try to make them *see* the thing as a kind of psychological challenge to them—that they should see Our Lord not as a doctrine but as a Person.

Take again—as a sort of combination of being soaked in dogma and soaked in New Testament—the famous objection of the street corner heckler to the infallibility of the Pope, that "Christ called Peter Satan." In our early years on the platform, we gave a thoroughly unsatisfactory answer to the question, an answer we had got out of the books. Our answer was this: Christ did say to St. Peter: "Get thee behind me, Satan"; but, we said, the context explains it. Our Lord had told the Apostles that He must go to Jerusalem to suffer and die. Peter, out of his love for our Lord, begged Him not to do so, and our Lord then said to Peter: "Get thee behind me, Satan"; and we explained that the word Satan means tempter and that Peter, out of love of our Lord, was tempting Him not to go through His suffering. And all this was very much to Peter's credit. That was our explanation and it never satisfied the crowd. Why? Because we had explained the words, but we had not explained the violence of the words. Satan does mean a tempter, but Satan means Satan: our Lord knew it, and Peter knew it, and it was a scarifying thing for our Lord to have said to Peter. Why the vehemence, if that was all? Go forward to the Agony in the Garden and you see more profoundly. Our Lord asks His Father the very thing that Peter had suggested to Him. "Don't make Me go through with this suffering." And our Lord feels the anguish of it, so that the sweat runs off like blood. Now, that sweat as of blood is the measure of the temptation that Peter is exposing our Lord

to, when he begged Him not to suffer and die. And once you
see the sweat as of blood, then you understand the vehemence
of "Get thee behind me, Satan."

Take one other example. You can remind your students
how every life is fed by its own kind, and cannot otherwise
be fed. If you want to feed your bodies, you must persuade
some animal to part with a little of its body—some cow to
sacrifice a steak, a lamb to sacrifice a chop. The body has
to be fed upon matter. If you want to feed your minds, it
is no good offering them chops: they must be fed on minds,
you must find someone with a richer mind and either by
getting him to talk to you, or by reading the book he has
written, you feed your mind on his mind, and your mind
grows in richness. But there is another life—the supernatural
life—and our Lord said that this life is Himself: "I *am* the
Life."—If there is a life that *is* Christ, and if every life must
be fed upon its like, the only food for a life which is Christ
is the Food which is Christ. And so you get the Blessed
Sacrament.

(ii) A most useful way with the class, when you have
done your uttermost to help them see what the doctrine is *in
itself,* is to get them to show, both to you and themselves in
one act, *what it would mean if the dogma were not there.*
Get them to search their minds with absolute honesty to see
what it would mean to themselves if this thing were not so,
then to generalize and see what it would mean to mankind.
Get them thinking about it, and talking about it. Of course,
in almost every dogma class, the major part of the talking
should be done by the pupils, guided by the teacher. It is a
great thing to get them accustomed to talking easily, freely,
and as the most natural thing in the world, upon Religion.
It will stand them in good stead, when they go out into the
world, if they have acquired this habit. And it will do an
immense amount for a world which is perishing for the want

of the very truths we could bring, if only we would learn to utter them, if only we would learn to say even a little of what we see. As part of this, children should be encouraged to raise the difficulties that occur to their minds. They have not always been much encouraged in this matter. Take the child who suddenly asks "Who made God?" Boys have told me what happened. Either they were punished for irreverence or they were wept over. They should, of course, have been rewarded, because they were using their minds on one of the great truths.

One way and another, what all this comes to is this: you are trying to give them a mental framework for reality, in which they can live healthily and grow in knowledge and love. They are going out into the world, and they are going to have all sorts of vital experiences which will test the framework—not simply intellectual objections against the Faith, but the sufferings and temptations which no one can avoid.

We must do all that lies in us to see that the framework is so strong and so true that none of life's experiences will ever succeed in smashing through it. The mark of a true framework is that it is stronger for the testing.

ON TEACHING
THE KEY DOCTRINES

*I am adding this Note, which
was not in the original talk, partly to answer questions asked
by teachers, but also for parents who may want to co-operate
in the religious education of their young. To teach the doctrines one must know them. Teachers, of course, will have
the necessary doctrinal formation, but parents may not. I
have treated all the points I am about to list in two books—
A MAP OF LIFE and (in much more detail) THEOLOGY
AND SANITY. For the parents of younger children, I mention Marigold Hunt's ST. PATRICK'S SUMMER (see page
26, below).*

Let us look more closely at our four-point master plan—
what God is, what man is, what Christ is, what union is. And
may I say once more that it is not for me, but for the teacher,
to say at what age this or that truth can be taught? My plea
is that the Catholic out in the world, and under pressure from
the world and the flesh and the devil, should know all these
truths and see them as central, relating to them all else that
he knows. He needs them in the world: he should not leave
school without them.

A Preliminary Note on Spirit

Involved in all four doctrines is the concept of spirit: it is *the* key to their understanding, as to the understanding of all religion. The mind which has not mastered its use cannot make much of what the Church has to tell. I must confess that, though I have been teaching Catholic doctrine these thirty years, it is only in the last few years that I have come to see this quite obvious fact as a first principle. If we are serious about teaching religion, we must concentrate upon spirit, always thinking of ways to make the idea clearer to the pupils, never satisfied that we have found the unimprovable method. *Spirit is not just one more topic in the long list of topics to be taught in religion class, it is basic to every topic;* it is not simply something to be known, but something without which nothing else can be known—at once an object of study in its own right, and a tool without which the mind cannot make progress—they must see it, and see *by* it. Thus it is not simply a matter of their learning and memorizing a definition, or even solely of mastering the meaning, but of acquiring a skill. Spirit should be as familiar a concept to them as their breakfast, and any amount of labour must be put into making it so. They will not understand God, or man, or Christ, or union, if they do not know what spirit is. If we are to grasp our own faith, and help others to do the same, we must be clear about spirit; no one should emerge from a Catholic school at any age, even if he emerges at fourteen, who has not been helped, to the limit of his and his teacher's capacity, to know what spirit is, so that he can handle it as an idea of which he sees the meaning and knows the importance.

It is, of course, difficult for the pupil; but the difficulty must not be exaggerated. The teacher has to work hard at preparing the lesson, and patiently at giving it, indeed it is a special test of the teacher's skill. The first step, anyhow, is no great problem. A child is very early aware that his body does not know or love, finds no difficulty in thinking of these as operations of his soul, and accepting the notion that knowing and loving go with being a spirit. Very early too he can realize that spirit has power, it can master matter and make matter serve it.

The next step is to introduce him to the idea of spirit as *permanent*. He can see that material things are changing, always liable to become something else, of any material thing other things can be made. He need not find it hard to grasp the idea that spirit is the very reverse of all this—it cannot become something else, nothing else can be made of it, it can only be itself; and, in my own experience, quite young children can be interested in the underlying reason for this difference between matter and spirit: material things can suffer change because they are composed of parts, and what has parts can be taken apart. Spirit has no parts, and therefore cannot be changed into anything else. Even a few minutes meditation on this by a class can work a profound change in their understanding.

A spirit has no parts, there is no element in it that is not the whole of it. They will not possess this idea at first meeting, but it will grow. As it does, they are ready for one further step: they can be helped to see how the possession of parts goes with occupying space, how therefore a spirit, having no parts, is superior to the need for space. (Neither upon this matter, nor the others I mention as I go along, am I bothering you with detail of teaching method; your own experience will tell you how, and at what age, to convey these truths.)

Just as their first awareness of spirit as permanent can be developed through the years, so can their first awareness of spirit as knowing and loving. These ideas must be further analyzed, to distinguish them as human and spiritual from animal imitations. Certainly by sixteen or seventeen they can have been taught the whole concept of spirit as the being which has a permanent hold upon its own nature, simple, outside space, the abiding reality under the endless changingness of matter, and again as a being of power, knowledge and love.

All this may seem obvious. But the adult Catholics one meets do not, by and large, know it or get any light from it. How can the next generation of adults, your generation of children, be helped to? It seems to me only by the teacher keeping the concept of spirit continuously before her mind as one into which her pupils must be continuously growing. It must be returned to constantly. In every year the ideas involved in it, *as stateable,* will be growing clearer and richer. Not only that: spirit itself will have been *lived with,* leading to an intimacy with the idea deeper than words or concepts can express. Spirit can become an essential element in the world they are mentally living in, so that world and thinking alike would seem miserably thin and impoverished without it, materialism however persuasively presented would at once be seen as repulsive and find all their mental habits ranged solidly against it: just as, if a man has learnt to walk, the most persuasive arguments could not get him to resort to crawling —he would find the idea repulsive, all his bodily habits would be ranged against it. The analogy is close—the mind that is aware of spirit is walking upright, the matter-bound mind crawls.

GOD

To the idea of spirit and its independence of space they can, even quite young, be shown how to join the ideas of eternity and infinity, and see God as the Infinite Eternal Spirit.

Infinite first, seen as greatness without limit. Every spirit has power, knowledge and love. The pupil can be reminded of his own limitations in all three—and it is no bad spiritual exercise that he be forced to concentrate on them, list the more obvious of them, see where he can extend the limits by developing his ability and his knowledge and his love, and where he will come to limits beyond which he cannot in any event pass. He is now able to attach some sort of meaning to the limitless power (so great, for example, that He can *make* things, using no material at all), the limitless knowledge and the limitless love of God.

Just as one approaches infinity by way of a concentration upon the limitations of the finite, so one approaches eternity by way of a concentration upon the "successiveness" of time. Provided we choose our vocabulary and our illustrations carefully, they can see that no one of us creatures here below is *all he is, all at once:* that if we consider ourselves, there is not only what we are now, but also what we used to be, and what we are not yet but one day will be; no one of us is at any moment all there. They can be familiarized with the fleetingness of our present, the word "now" applying to a different moment every time we use it, indeed not remaining present even while we are saying it (for while we are saying the n-, the -ow is still in the future, while we are saying the -ow, the n- has already vanished in the past). One way or another, by having considered the various ways in which no one of us is *all he is, all at once,* they can grow into easy familiarity with the phrase. Once they are thus familiar with it, they can be told that it *is* true of God, God is *all He is, all at once* (that indeed being Boethius' classic definition of eternity). God then knows infinitely and loves infinitely, none of His knowing or loving vanishes away into a past, there is no future from which any more knowing and loving can come to Him, because He already does both limitlessly.

As the years go by, this refining process in the ideas of spirit, infinite, eternal can continue. It will be for the teacher to decide at what age the various steps can be taken; but as a

general principle it may be agreed that the earlier the pupil
is helped to take the first steps, the sooner he will be ready for
the later developments. Certainly it is an enlargement and a
liberation for the minds of the young to see time, as they have
already seen space, as not of the essence of all conceivable being, however much it be bound up with the kind of being we
are. So early it can be only a seed, the glimpse of a possibility,
but nurtured it will grow.

To have brought them to a better than verbal acquaintance
with God as Infinite Eternal Spirit is a great thing, great in
itself and the necessary preparation for a better than verbal
acquaintance with the Blessed Trinity. They have seen God,
infinite and eternal, *knowing* infinitely. They can now be told
how in that infinite knowing He produces the infinitely perfect thought of Himself, a thought which is not only something
(as our thoughts are) but Someone, equal to Himself in all
perfections, the Son, the Second Person; and how Father and
Son, loving infinitely, produce a total lovingness within the
Godhead, a lovingness which is not only something (as ours
is) but Someone, possessing all the perfections of Father and
Son, for they have poured their all into it. In my own experience, it is better thus to begin with the processions of Son and
Holy Ghost and when these truths are really living in the
mind, go on to show what we mean by person and what by
nature, and why what they have just learned is summarized as
Three Persons in One God.

But how early can the effort to lead them into the mystery
of the Trinity be made? Earlier, perhaps, than is always realized. The small child finds the doctrine in some ways easier
than the adult: his power to accept reality has not been hard-
ened and stiffened by routine and the customary as ours has:
it does not bother him to be told of a thought that is not only
Something but Someone. Yet that is not the only, or the main,
consideration. Return, for a moment, to the view of teaching

as a dialogue between the Holy Ghost in the teacher and the Holy Ghost in the child. You are not teaching merely natural intellects. These children have been baptized. The Blessed Trinity indwells them. If ever the Holy Ghost can be relied on to help, it must surely be upon this truth. The child can hinder Him by any of the countless ways of cussedness open to the young. The teacher can hinder Him by not giving the whole power of her mind to the seeing and the saying of the truth. A slackly prepared lesson on God is one way of taking God's name in vain. This matter of teaching the doctrine of the Blessed Trinity is the classic example of the maxim "Work as if everything depended on you, pray as if everything depended on God." After all, you are the people who KNOW HOW TO TEACH; and I am convinced that if you bring all your wealth of teaching experience to bear upon ways of introducing the child to the Trinity, advances will be made by which the whole Church will be the gainer. Meanwhile a pioneering work of extraordinary value has been done by Marigold Hunt in St. Patrick's Summer. This book is an exposition of Catholic dogma directed at ten-year-olds. In the story, St. Patrick instructs them upon the Blessed Trinity—expounding it stage by stage, at each stage getting them to tell it back to him, correcting them, drawing them on to the next stage. It is really brilliant pedagogy.

MAN

Once again, it is for the practised teacher to decide what can be taught when; but, by the time the pupil leaves school, he should have the following truths about man so mastered that, in all his thinking of himself and others, they operate automatically, so to speak.

(i) He will of course have been taught that Man is made by God of nothing. It is essential that he be shown slowly and patiently and unforgettably (a large word, I know, when the young are in question) how it follows from this that he could not continue in existence, unless God continued to hold him, that he is held in existence from moment to moment only because God wills to hold him there. This is one of those realities, like spirit, which cannot simply be taught and left. *It is as basic to the understanding of man, as spirit to the understanding of everything.* If it becomes part of the pupil's very consciousness, he will see everything differently—more as it truly is than merely as it looks. For one example, it will take a lot of the bounce out of him to know that he is made of nothing, that God is holding him there and that if God dropped him, so to speak, he would be back in his native nothingness in no time at all: it is good for him to know that he himself, like everything else in creation, is expressed in that formula. For another example, he will see sin as folly—for sin means trying to gain something against the will of God: but only the will of God holds us in existence at all: what could be more idiotic? The realization may not stop anyone from sinning, but, if we must sin, it is better that we feel fools while doing it.

(ii) But if it is vital that the pupil should know his nothingness compared with God, he should also know his, and every man's, splendour simply as man. He should be aware of the greater splendour of the soul, as spiritual and immortal, made by God in His own image, and of the lesser splendour of the body as God's handiwork. He should be shown what it means for the splendour of both that God became man and took to Himself a human soul and a human body; and what it adds to the value of all men that Christ our Lord died to redeem them. This picture of man—as a union of matter and spirit, by his spirit immortal and in God's image, redeemed by Christ—should become so much part of his thinking that he can never see himself or any other man without seeing him so, can never make a decision about himself or another without taking it into account.

(iii) He must also have some notion of what is meant by the union of matter and spirit—of its strangeness first of all, given that matter is in space and spirit not, and then of the mode of it. By the time he is old enough, he can be given the notion of spirit pouring out its forming and animating energies upon the body, so that no part of the body lacks them (that being the sense in which the soul is in every part of the body). Younger, he may be helped by some such comparison as water boiling over a flame—the flame not in the same space as the water, yet by its heating energies in every part of the water all the same: the water so obvious, hissing and steaming and spilling over, the flame so still, that a chance spectator might think the water was everything and overlook the flame altogether (as there are people who think the body is everything and deny that there is a soul).

(iv) He should have been helped to meditate on the concept of man as a rational animal: especially on the truth—of which he, like all of us, has continuing experience—that rational does not mean reasonable but only endowed with reason, a reason he may use or misuse, that man is not only the one animal that can act reasonably but the one animal that can act unreasonably. There are all sorts of ways in which the teacher can profitably set the class musing on themselves as rational animals.

CHRIST OUR LORD

What Christ is means the dogma of Incarnation, but in addition to that, it means a personal intimacy with Christ our Lord. I am not sure that that would not be the starting point of learning everything; everything has to be built up from that. Now I need not tell you that a personal intimacy is something one has to acquire for oneself. You cannot hand on your personal intimacy with someone to someone else. He has to get it for himself. Intimacy is not the same for any two people. You and I might each know a third person most intimately. The third person himself might be unable to say which of us is the closer friend. Yet each of us would have a really different picture of the person—not different in every way, of course, but different in a great many things. No one is able to respond to all the qualities of any other person; some respond to some, and some to others. I might respond to his love for Shakespeare. You might respond to his love for Bach, which would not mean a thing to me. But if there is no human being to every quality of whom one human person can respond, immeasurably more so is that true of Christ our Lord, and of course of our Lady in a lesser degree. We all respond to different elements in Christ, but we have to find them for ourselves. The student, like the teacher, should be soaked in the Gospels. He cannot meet our Lord anywhere else, not as He lived and moved and talked: that is where He is. St. Jerome said, in the fifth century, and Pope Benedict XV in the twentieth made the phrase his own, that "ignorance of the Scriptures is ignorance of Christ." And as a kind of corollary of that, the ignoring of the Scriptures really looks like a lack of interest in Christ our Lord. It seems unthinkable that we should love Him and not want to know more about Him, know all that we possibly could about him.

This knowing about Him means, as we have just seen, *meeting* Him as He lived and acted among men and knowing the detail of His earthly life. But it also means knowing who and what He was, the dogma of the Incarnation in short. Where the Trinity has been carefully studied it is all much easier. The pupils will already be familiar with the concepts of person and nature, by attaching a meaning to three persons in one nature, will have seen that one person to one nature is not the only possible proportion, so to speak, and will be prepared therefore for the dogma of one person with two natures. It is vital here to make them realize that while the nature decides what actions are possible, it is the person who does them; thus that, because Christ had a human nature, He could perform genuinely human actions, yet the He who performed them was God the Son. This is not simply a theologi-. cal technicality; as we have already noted, our redemption depends upon it. It was God the Son who was born of the Virgin Mary, it was God the Son who died on the cross, in each case, of course, in His human nature, not in His divine nature.

UNION

We have glanced at the three—God, men, Christ—whose union defines the Church. It remains to see what their union means.

(i) *Just as the key to the understanding of religion as a whole is spirit, and to the understanding of all creatures, man included, is God's conserving action, so the key to the understanding of the union of men with God in Christ is Sanctifying Grace.* And in the same way as spirit and God's continuing maintenance of man in being, grace must be taught continuously, the teacher must concentrate intensely on ways of making the doctrine known, realized, part of the very structure of the mind. I speak with some feeling: until well into my twenties, all I knew of Grace was that it was something to die in a state of. The Church simply cannot be understood without it, everything she does is done that we may have Grace and increase it. Experience seems to show that the young grasp it best as Supernatural Life—in the gradation life, natural, supernatural. Thus they can be helped to see it as a new set of powers, in the soul, enabling man to do things that by his natural powers alone he could not do, things that he must be able to do if he is (a) to attain heaven (b) to live there. They can see Grace operating here as faith, hope and charity, and finding its full flowering in the Beatific Vision: this, too, with careful, patient teaching can—must—be made a reality to the pupils, otherwise they will not know what that heaven is towards which their whole life must be directed: one always moves more languidly to a cloudy goal. Grace is union with God here below, heaven is union achieved, total, final: just as sin is refusal of union, and hell is refusal definitive, chosen eternally.

(ii) The breach made by sin between the human race and God was closed by Christ's redemptive passion and death; it is in union with Him that we are to be united to God. The truth that the Church is Christ's mystical Body has three consequences for union

(a) Life, supernatural life, flows from Christ to us, making us one body with Him, incorporating us with Him (roughly on the analogy of the cells in any living body) so that He lives in us and we in Him; we are more closely related to Him in the order of grace than even His Mother was in the order of nature—though she, of course, is immeasurably closer to Him in grace than we shall ever be;

(b) united with Him, we are necessarily united with His heavenly Father—"I in my father and you in me";

(c) in the shared life of one body men are related not only to Christ the Head (though this is primary) but also to one another, and more closely than by *any* natural relationship: we are closer than brothers, we are members one of another. Even an *attempt* to live up to this truth would revolutionize social life.

Christ's life flows to us in the Body by way of the Sacraments: the Blessed Sacrament, above all. In the Body Christ continues to offer Himself once slain upon Calvary to His heavenly Father for the application to men individually of the rich treasure He merited for the whole race of man on Calvary. In the Body, we receive His truth infallibly—"we have the mind of Christ."

(iii) The Church then is Christ our Lord continuing to do through a body of men the same truth-giving, life-giving work that He did in His own natural Body while He was on earth. But the Church has a human side too, and the young should be shown the implications of this long before they leave school; otherwise their faith is going to be tried very bitterly. What Christ has *guaranteed* in the Church—truth without any alloy of error, life by way of the sacraments—is perfect. What the human members of the Church, from Popes to laymen, do on their own judgment varies from the highest sanctity to the lowest depths of sin. It is a wicked thing to leave children to find this out from the Church's enemies when they have left school. Indeed it is a black mark against a school if the pupils meet, in the world outside, objections for which they were not prepared in school: obviously they cannot be told of every objection and its answer, but there are certain main categories into which objections fall and they can be introduced to these. They should, one feels, be prepared as for a mixed marriage—which would certainly reduce the number of mixed marriages. It is plain common-sense that they should hear of the objections in school, where they can be given the answers as well, rather than left to hear the objections, without the answers, in the outer world. On this matter of what is called Scandals—varying from great crimes down to ordinary human failings—it is especially urgent that they should learn in school. Otherwise, when they hear them outside, they may begin by denying them and suffer the humiliation of defeat in a needless battle; and their faith may be shaken by a feeling that their teachers never mentioned these things because the Church is afraid of them. They will on this matter, at least, be unshakable if (a) they have been taught that the Church depends on Christ's holiness, not on men's; and (b) they realize that they are in the Church for the sake of the gifts of Truth and Life

which Christ gives in it, *not* for the sake of the men through
whom Christ gives them: the essential thing they get from
the Church is union with our Lord to the level of their willingness to be united.

A General Note on Mystery

Before embarking on this rapid tour of the four elements in
the definition of the Church, I talked of spirit as the foundation concept. Now at the end of it, something must be said
of Mystery as the atmosphere in which all must be seen.
Seeing reality is an exhilarating experience; but part of seeing it consists in seeing why we cannot see more of it. There
is a first stage of sheer ignorance in which nothing is seen:
the darkness is simply darkness. Then the light of revelation
is given and a new universe comes into view. But our minds
are limited, there are realities beyond man's vision, even his
grace-aided vision; and once more there is darkness. But it
need not be simply darkness: if we know *why* we can see no
further, the darkness is a sort of light, and we shall not be
irked at not being omniscient. The young should be constantly aware that Mystery is inescapable—mystery in the
form of truths we cannot see how to reconcile with each
other, mystery in the even more testing form of happenings
we cannot see how to reconcile with God's goodness. None
of these things need be dangerous, they may indeed be enriching, to the mind which is livingly aware of its own limitations and God's limitless knowledge and love—knowledge
which means that God sees where men cannot, love which
means that men can trust God unquestioningly.

As I think back over this outline, I know that every element in it is already being taught. I cannot imagine any
Syllabus anywhere that would omit any of it (except, perhaps, the scandals). It is all being taught. But it is not being
learnt—learnt, that is, in the sense of still being vivid and

operative in the mind of Catholics ten years out of school.
Let me remind you once more that I am basing all I have to
say in this paper, *not* on what happens in school but on what
remains in the mind afterwards, not on the process of religious education but on the product. I think it may be a matter
of proportion, of light and shade. Teaching the faith does
not mean simply teaching one thing after another till the list
of things teachable is exhausted. The young must be given
the shape of reality, with the elements emphasized that matter
most—either in themselves, as Trinity, Incarnation and Beatific Vision, or as keys to the understanding of these great
matters. Reality, seen thus in its true shape, should be ever
growing in clarity and so in grip on the mind. Other truths
must, of course, be taught, for I am not here drawing up a
Syllabus of Religious Instruction; but they will be best learnt
in their place in the master-plan, enriching it but never al-
lowed to obscure its main lines. The difficulty of all learning
is the difficulty of seeing the wood for the trees: in this
subject it is almost a tragedy.

Where, in all this, comes piety? It may seem that I am
suggesting a purely intellectual instruction, with will and
emotions left on one side. Partly this arises from my own
position as a layman: I am not equipped to give you guid-
ance upon the development of your students' spiritual lives:
nor, upon that, do you lack guides. Yet, as I have said, that
is only part of the story. The truth is that the will and the
emotions will re-act best to truths seen truly. A teacher can
set about exciting devotion to our Lord, the Mass and the
Blessed Eucharist, Our Lady: but unless the young know—
to the limit of their power of grasping what the Church has
to teach them—what those realities are *in themselves,* how
can their reaction to them be genuine? All too easily the reaction of the impressionable young is not to the doctrines at
all, but to the teacher's reaction to the doctrines: *their* emo-

tional response is rooted in hers, not in the realities; and all too often today the reaction goes the other way, they dislike an enthusiasm which seems to them meaningless, and doctrine and teacher are involved in one single rejection. They must, then, as we all must, study the doctrines not for the sake of the emotional vibrations they may stir but to find out what they mean. The vibrations will come of themselves. Between stimulated reactions and simulated the gap is not wide.